# DAWN

---

# FRENCH

## A Detailed Biography

John Brooklyn

# Table of Contents

# Young Dawn

D awn Roma French was born on October 11th, 1957 in Holyhead, Wales. Her parents, Felicity Roma and Denys Vernon French, who were both born in England, got married in Plymouth in 1953. French has an elder sibling called Gary. Her father served in the RAF and was stationed at RAF Valley and RAF Leconfield. In her comedy tour/video, Thirty Million Minutes, French included old footage of *Queen Elizabeth The Queen Mother* visiting their home when she was three years old.

She received financial assistance from the *Royal Air Force* to support her private education. During her father's time at *RAF Faldingworth*, she attended *Caistor Grammar* School. She later enrolled at St. Dunstan's Abbey School for Girls in Plymouth, which is no longer operational. During her time at St. Dunstan's, French lived in Downton. Following her high school graduation, she utilized a debate scholarship to attend the Spence School in New York for a year.

French says her father's constant affirmations of her attractiveness were essential in helping her develop a strong sense of identity. Denys was depressed, but he kept his sickness a secret from Dawn and Gary.

French's father committed suicide while she was just 19 years old.

When Dawn French joined the acting program at the prestigious Royal Central School of Speech and Acting in 1977, she crossed paths with Jennifer Saunders, who would later become her comedic partner. Surprisingly, despite both being RAF veterans and growing up on the same base, they had never really interacted before. At their initial meeting, French came across as an arrogant newcomer, while Saunders seemed snobbish and distant. It's amusing to think about now, but their initial clash stemmed from French's ambition to become a theatre teacher, a career choice that Saunders strongly disapproved of. French resented

Saunders for her unwavering enthusiasm and confidence in pursuing that particular path.

French and Saunders lived together in a student apartment, where they were encouraged to take comedic writing seriously for their final projects. They became buddies after a particularly in-depth talk between them. In the meanwhile, French and her fiancé, a former Royal Navy officer, broke up. After graduating from the Royal Central School, French and Saunders took the risky step of forming the duo act Menopause Sisters. Saunders has jokingly called their performance *cringeworthy* since they wore tampons in their ears. This routine, however, is what brought French and Saunders to the forefront of the comic world as members of the

Comic Strip in the early 1980s.

The Life of Dawn French

# The Comic Journey

In 1982, Dawn French made her first appearance on television in *The Comic Strip Presents* on Channel 4, marking the start of her successful career in front of the camera. Her debut film role was in a comedic adaptation of Enid Blyton's Famous Five novels called *Five Go Mad in Dorset*.

In this parody, French played the role of *George*, a family member of *Julian*, *Anne*, and their canine companion *Timmy*. The plot centers around the children's vacation at the residence of their *Uncle Quentin* and *Aunt Fanny*. However, the situation takes an unforeseen twist when they unearth the shocking revelation that Uncle Quentin has been abducted.

Despite this unexpected situation, the *Five* refuse to be discouraged and opt to carry on with their vacation by exploring Dorset on bicycles. During their journey, they enjoy a picnic and unexpectedly come across a group of criminals, whom they immediately inform the authorities about. Appreciating their bravery, *Robbie Coltrane's* character, the *grocer*, rewards them with scrumptious pastries.

Inside the store, they encounter *Daniel Peacock's* obnoxious and spoiled character, *Toby*. Initially, the kids are put off by *Toby's* irritating behavior and their sense of superiority, so they choose to avoid spending time with him. However, the plot takes a surprising twist when *Toby* himself is abducted, leading to a change in events.

This time around, *Coltrane* is portrayed as a sleazy gypsy. *The Five* discover a hidden tunnel that takes them to an abandoned castle where they meet *Toby*. They also unexpectedly found *Uncle Quentin*, who admits that he was kidnapped as part of a plot to hide the fact that he and *Aunt Fanny* had split up because of his homosexuality. Upon promptly realizing the gravity of the situation, the children swiftly contact the authorities, consequently resulting in the apprehension of Uncle Quentin.

The satirical film *Five Go Mad in Dorset* pokes fun at the sexism, racism, and elitism that permeate *Enid Blyton's Famous Five* series. The video also makes light of the repetitive nature of children's adventure tales. Among the recurrent jokes are allusions to ginger beer and the protagonist's penchant for lavish feasts. The term *lashings of ginger beer* became popular despite never appearing in any of Blyton's works. The 30-minute presentation also drew attention to the illegality of homosexuality in Britain before 1968 and the apparent love bond between *George* and her dog *Timmy*. Even though the broadcaster got permission from *Blyton's* estate, complaints were filed about the allusions and mocking in *Five Go Mad in Dorset*.

Despite receiving accolades for its spot-on parody, the show was also compared poorly to another program with the same name. Despite suffering from acute tonsillitis for a portion of the shoot, *Jennifer Saunders* recalls the experience fondly in her 2013 book. She remembers that period as the happiest since the group used their per diem money to have a good time at a bar.

*Comic Strip Presents* included *French and Saunders*, as well as regulars *Peter Richardson, Rik Mayall, Nigel Planer, Robbie Coltrane, and Adrian Edmondson,* each in his own stories. She had a hand in 27 out of the 37 episodes as an actor and two as a writer. The first episode was a spoof of spaghetti westerns, while the second was a black-and-white comedy about a youngster who can't stop being a doofus. Comic producer Martin Lewis released a record album in 1981 called Comic Strip, which included many routines by French and his frequent comic partner, Jennifer Saunders. French and Jennifer Saunders were introduced to listeners outside of London with the publication of this album by Springtime!/Island Records in September 1981.

In the British comedy series *The Young Ones*, French made a brief appearance as a mentally unstable Christian woman. The following year, she starred in the 1985 release *Girls on Top* along with *Saunders, Ullman, and Wax*. The film revolves around four unique women who live together in a London apartment.

The series starred French as *Amanda*, a young lady in her twenties who is unable to pay the rent on a property she is given by *Lady Carlton* (*Joan Greenwood*). Since *Candice* (*Tracey*) has nowhere else to go, she manages to persuade *Amanda* to let her remain in the apartment temporarily. *Jennifer* (*Saunders*), an old acquaintance of Amanda's, then shows up. Amanda eventually lets Shelley into her apartment, and the two of them end up sharing the rent since no one else can afford it to save Amanda and her affluent family.

Later episodes focused on Shelley imposing her will on the others since they depended on her to have the rent paid, while early episodes often featured

Candice's newest fabricated sickness or any other excuse to not pay the rent.

During the period from October 1985 to December 1986, the TV series *Happy Families* had two complete seasons. This country comedy-drama featured *Jennifer Saunders and Dawn French* in prominent roles and was set in that time frame. The show revolves around a hilariously dysfunctional family sitcom, with characters like *Granny Fuddle (played by Jennifer Saunders), Cook (played by Dawn French), and Idiot Grandson (played by Adrian Edmondson)*. A significant storyline in the series is *Guy's* quest to find his four sisters so that they can reunite. Each sister's story is portrayed in a different genre, including a serious

BBC documentary, a *funny Ealing farce*, and a *lighthearted* American *soap opera*. Eventually, the family is brought back together, but they discover that their grandmother has always harbored hatred towards them and only brought them together to use their organs for a transplant. However, the procedure is interrupted when *Granny* Fuddle reveals she is pregnant! In the final episode, *Guy* plans to marry *Flossy*, the maid, and the family agrees to provide their grandmother with a monthly allowance so she can care for the newborn uncle. Additionally, Dawn French briefly played the role of an evil sibling in an episode of *The Story Teller*.

# French & Saunders

Dawn French and Jennifer Saunders started working together in comedy after meeting in theater school. Their dedication and skill helped them rise to fame when they appeared in many episodes of *The Comic Strip Presents...* At this point, French and Saunders joined forces with many other aspiring performers and comedians in the underground comedy movement.

They performed in an edition of *The Entertainers on Channel 4* in 1983. On the same network's weekly music show, *The Tube*, they also offered some much-needed comic relief. French made headlines at the moment because he used a specific phrase on British television for the first time. The duo's comic talents were further acknowledged in 1986 when they began making recurring appearances for Comic Relief. The BBC recognized their abilities and signed them to a multiyear deal.

French and Saunders introduced their innovative sketch comedy show in 1987. Viewers were enthralled by this series for a span of six seasons and nine specials, lasting until 2005. Even after the show concluded, collections of their earlier work continued to bring joy to audiences, extending to 2017. The film, beginning with modest origins, ultimately became a remarkable success in the world of comedy.

The first season was made to seem like a cheap variety show by purposefully having the protagonists do risky, usually unsuccessful, things. To make matters worse, esteemed actors were deliberately subjected to mistreatment. *Simon Brint* and *Rowland Rivron*, portraying *Ken* and *Duane Bishop*, formed a musical duo named *Raw*, with one playing bongos and the other on the keyboard. Additionally, there was a group of elderly dancers known as *The Hot Hoofers*. Notably, *Alison Moyet* and *Joan Armatrading* made appearances on separate episodes as special guests. This type of light entertainment program required a broader range of content beyond just comedy, which is why incorporating dance and music was crucial. This decision was driven by the fact that the BBC's Light Entertainment department had a larger budget compared to their Comedy division. In the second season (1988), the concept of a show within the show was abandoned.

The show's popularity increased with time, and in 1994, BBC decided to promote it from BBC2 to BBC1. To construct their elaborate parodies of popular culture, French and Saunders were given higher resources. Movies including *Thelma & Louise*, *Titanic*, *Misery*, and *What Ever Happened to Jane?* were reenacted, while *Madonna*, *Bananarama*, *ABBA*, and *The Corrs* were lampooned in musical parodies. As a special gift for their devoted audience, the comic pair often recycled lines and visual gags from older pieces. Their inability to successfully mimic regional dialects became a running joke. The argument over their Southern accents first appeared in a *Gone with the Wind spoof*. A heavy Northern Irish accent was the result of French's effort at the accent. Since then, they have taken several breaks throughout their skits to double-check their accents and recite the lines.

The program cleverly used references to itself to remind viewers that they were watching a parody. Unlike typical parodies, French and Saunders relied on the audience's understanding to enhance the humor.

The Life of Dawn French

In its last season, which aired in 2004, the show circled back to its metafictional roots. In this segment, the two comics mocked their inability to get anything done. Saunders subsequently said that this was a realistic depiction of their writing process, as they were coming up with ideas for their writing during what seemed like procrastination to outsiders. The sitcom also featured a fictitious version of *Liza Tarbuck* serving as producer despite her desire to instead develop and create game shows. *Lorna Brown* also played *Abba*, the production assistant. Their agent, *Mo* (played by *Maggie Steed*), was modeled by the real-life *Maureen Vincent*, who appeared in two episodes. *Abba's* visions of French

**24** | P a g e

and Saunders as old ladies also included short visits from *Eileen Essell* and *Brenda Cowling*. In 2005, French and Saunders concluded their series with a Christmas special. Two years later, in 2007, a compilation of their episodes titled *A Bucket of French and Saunders* was broadcast.

French's sudden departure from the sketch program in 2004 caught Saunders and their loyal fan base by surprise, despite the duo's obvious success. In 2023, French finally gave an interview in which she explained her abrupt departure. She said that she decided to quit the program after a particularly difficult day of shooting left her feeling ugly and she cried hot, furious tears.

*French and Saunders*, a comedy pair, were in the BBC office on that fatal day, working on a skit. French tells her in the scenario that she hopes to get the attention of American popstar Anastacia and be asked to sing on Top of the Pops. They had no idea what twist destiny had in store for them.

They didn't know that Anastacia was eavesdropping on their talk from behind the stalls. Soon, French found herself wearing Anastacia's trademark cowgirl outfit and singing on *Top of the Pops with the star*. But she felt no happiness, only a crushing self-doubt. She had never felt so unattractive as she did at that moment.

French has shown throughout her career that she was prepared to adopt unfavorable looks if it would make for better humor. As long as it contributed to the comedy, it never worried her previously. It hurt when she saw her reflection in the mirror and knew the joke was on her.

French casually departed the studio when the day's shooting was over. After she got in her vehicle, though, she started crying hot, furious tears. She felt the weight of the unpleasant event, and she grieved the whole way home. She had no idea that French and Saunders would air its last episode that day.

In 2010, French and Saunders were featured in three two-hour radio programs on BBC Radio 2. The following year, they offered holiday-themed specials on *Easter* and the *Bank Holidays*. Then, in 2020, they made their podcast debut with a series called *French & Saunders: Titting About, exclusively available on Audible.* Each episode of the podcast features casual and sometimes sentimental conversations on various subjects. Due to the success of the first season, a second season was released in 2021, followed by a third season in 2022.

In 2021, the exciting news came that *Gold* had ordered a new one-off special starring French and Saunders titled *French and Saunders: Funny Women.* This episode was filmed on the set of their original sketch series and offers a thought-provoking debate hosted by French and Saunders about the incredible history of women who have made important contributions to the field of comedy. On July 17 of that year, Gold broadcast the program.

***

Going back to the '80s, French played Debbie Draws in the black comedy *Eat the Rich*, which was both bleak and hilarious.

To kick off the new decade, Dawn French took the spotlight in the darkly comedic series *Murder Most Horrid*, which ran from 1991 to 1999. Each week, she played a new character on the show, and occasionally she even played both the killer and the victim.

*Absolutely Fabulous* was a smashing success for French and her comedy partner Jennifer Saunders in 1992. The series follows the lives of *PR* tycoon *Edina Monsoon* and her ex-model best friend *Patsy Stone*. These two women are constantly trying to stay young and hip by engaging in risky behaviors like binge drinking, drug use, and following the latest fashion trends. Saffron, Edina's daughter, has the unenviable task of taking care of her immature mother.

While Saunders was one of the series's primary characters, French made a lasting impression in a guest role as interviewer *Kathy* in the first episode of *Absolutely Fabulous. Kathy*, a character played by

French, was a hilarious spoof of the popular *TV* host *Lorraine Kelly*. The program featuring *Kathy* aired from 1992 to 1996, then again from 2001 to 2004, and 2011 to 2012. In the movie, *Absolutely Fabulous* released in 2016, French reprised her role as Kathy but this time as an older and more experienced journalist, resembling the real-life *Lorraine Kelly*. Saunders and French have confirmed that there won't be any more episodes or a sequel to the film. After her appearance in *Absolutely Fabulous*, French also portrayed *Elaine Dobbs* in *Screen One* and lent her voice to the character *Jim Hawkins* in *The Legends of Treasure Island.*

*Richard Curtis's* long-running BBC comedy *The Vicar of Dibley,* in which Dawn French starred, is her most notable solo television appearance to date. After the Church of England opened the priesthood to women in 1993, the narrative of *Geraldine Granger*, a vicar in the made-up community of *Dibley*, began airing on television in 1994.

The BBC series *The Vicar of Dibley* has become one of the most popular shows in the United Kingdom since the advent of digital media. *Its holiday* and *New Year's Eve* specialties are always ranked among the best in the United Kingdom. In addition to being nominated for many *British Academy Television Awards,* the program has won several *British Comedy Awards* and two International *Emmys*. In reality, it was voted third-best *British sitcom in 2004* by the *BBC*.

There were 12.3 million people who tuned in to see French's character get married on the show's last full-length episode. When *Comic Relief* was formed in 2013, it included a special mini-episode of *The Vicar of Dibley* starring both *Damian Lewis* and *Rebecca French*. She was nominated for a *BAFTA* for *Best Comedy Performance* because of her work in the series' final episode.

The original run of *The Vicar of Dibley* ended in 2007, although replays of the show on BBC One continue to attract millions of people. Even among American PBS viewers, the program maintains a devoted fan base. In addition, the series will return for a total of four new episodes in December 2020. After the 2015

*Red Nose Day Special*, French showed an interest in resuming her role as *The Bishop of Dibley* in a new series. However, there have been no recent releases or announcements of a new series as of yet.

French had to deal with the tragic death of four co-stars from *The Vicar of Dibley*. Roger *Lloyd-Pack*, who played farmer *Owen Newitt*, died of pancreatic cancer in January 2014 at the age of 69, making him one of these victims. French held a touching 10-minute tribute on the BBC in honor of her co-star, praising him as a great, engaging, and complicated human being. She decided that screening the pilot episode of Only Fools and Horses, in which Lloyd-Pack also starred, was the finest way to honor his memory.

The death of gifted actress *Liz Smith* on Christmas Eve 2016 at the age of 95 was another tragic incident. Sadly, *Smith* passed away not long after the transmission of the series finale of *The Royle Family*, for which she was best remembered for her portrayal as *Dibley* church organist *Letitia Cropley* in the first series.

When *Emma* Chambers, 53, unexpectedly passed away in February 2018, the string of catastrophes continued. Popular for her depiction of the kind but dimwitted *Alice, Chambers* was also a real-life close friend of French's. Her untimely death, from what was believed to be a heart attack, devastated fans of her work.

Later that year in November, *John Bluthal*, 89, who portrayed the inept secretary of the Parish Council, *Frank Pickle*, died away. Emma was honored in that year's holiday episodes when Geraldine delivered a touching eulogy for her deceased friend *Alice* (*Emma's* character in the *Vicar* series), leaving *Hugo* (*James Fleet*) in tears. *Dawn* found the experience so genuine that she couldn't hold back her emotions during the shooting of the devastating sequences.

*Dawn* said the eulogy was incredibly important to her, but she still hasn't seen the heartbreaking incident. Dawn has promised an homage to the show's legendary post-credits moments, in which Geraldine tells Alice a joke she doesn't get.

In the 1995 *Comic Relief* skit titled *Dawn*, created by *Victoria Wood*, *Dawn French* played the role of a talk show presenter. *Celia Imrie, Lill Roughley, Anne Reid, Philip Lowrie, Robert Kingswell, Bryan Burdon, Duncan Preston, Jim Broadbent, and Lynda Bellingham* also appeared in the sketch with Wood.

There were more noteworthy appearances of French throughout the 1990s. She was the *Baker's Wife* in *The Adventures of Pinocchio* and a former employee in *Let Them Eat Cake*, a comedy from 1999. She also played Mrs. *Crupp* in the TV adaptation of *David Copperfield*.

French voiced Buttercup in the 2000 animated series *Watership Down*. She provided her voice for the show's narrator in the next year's iteration of *The Wheels on the Bus.* In the comedic flick Maybe, she plays *Charlene.* The story follows *Sam* and *Lucy*, a married couple having difficulty having a child. Despite suffering from writer's block, BBC commissioning editor Sam chooses to compose a screenplay about their position. He finds success with the film with the aid of Lucy's journal notes. When Lucy sees the movie, she is so upset that she dumps Sam. They can make up and keep trying to have a family. The film's low reception and box office results were unfortunately not a surprise.

French also had an appearance in the drama/comedy miniseries *Ted and Alice.* French portrayed a *Lake*

*District* tourist information worker who develops feelings for an extraterrestrial visitor. She also appeared in *Wild West*, a BBC comedy starring *Catherine Tate* and herself. In the program, the two lesbian characters owned and operated a general shop in a fictional *Cornish* village. The show followed the characters as they interacted with and were affected by members of the neighborhood. Each episode focused on a different problem and the characters' solutions to it. The series lasted for two years from 2002 to 2004, however, it was not as popular as her previous performances.

*Rosie* (*French*), a lady with dissociative identity disorder who also has an alias named *Margaret*

(French), had a pivotal part in *Jam & Jerusalem*. Several people in *Clatterford*, a fictional little town, are the focus of the episode. Sal *Vine*, a registered nurse, finds solace in the *Women's Guild* following the loss of her husband. Tip, her closest friend, aids in her return to the medical facility where she had worked. *Margaret, Rosie's* evil twin, is unpleasant and cruel, yet *Rosie* herself is a kind person. *Delilah* is the old organist at the church who has a knack for getting into sticky situations. *Eileen* is the *Women's Guild's* chairperson and has an arrogant demeanor. *Caroline*, an affluent mother of four, sometimes confuses one meaning of a word for another. After *Sal's* passing, his son, *Dr. James Vine* runs the family company. *Tash, Sal*'s younger daughter, is a brat who refuses to take responsibility for herself. *Verger* duties and lollipop distribution fall to *Queenie. Yasmeen, James*'s wife, gets hired as the clinic's new nurse. The vicar of the church where *The Vicar work*s is a grouch. *Kate* is a young widow and a fellow guild woman, yet she often feels alone. Friend and fellow Guild member *Susie* is a rich businesswoman. *Jennifer Saunders, Patrick Barlow, and Sue Johnston* co-starred with French in this series.

A surprise appearance was made by the star of French and Saunders in the show *Little Britain*, where she played the role of *Vicky Pollard*'s mom. Additionally, she took part in a *Comic Relief* episode of

*Little Britain Live*, which was broadcast on the BBC and featured various famous guests. In one skit, she appeared alongside *Daffyd* Thomas as a lesbian bartender.

French, known for her versatile acting skills, took on the role of *Janet Erskine* in the 2006 episode *Sleeping Murder* of *Agatha Christie's Marple*. She showcased her talent once again in 2008 when she portrayed *Caroline Arless* in the BBC series *Lark Rise* to *Candleford*, which was based on *Flora Thompson's* books. The series received critical acclaim and ran from 2008 until 2011, delighting viewers with its compelling storyline. Caroline's character was characterized by her upbeat and exuberant nature, often indulging in drinking, laughing, and singing. Despite her lively personality, she had a deep love for her family, even though they had a penchant for exaggeration.

She made guest appearances on *High Table* and *The Meaning* of *Life* in 2007. Before that, Dawn began presenting *Dawn French's Girls Who Do Comedy*, in which she spoke to well-known comics like *Phyllis Diller*, *Catherine Tate*, and *Whoopi Goldberg* about their professions and lifestyles. Six comedians were interviewed for the series, first in excerpt form and subsequently in their entirety. *Dawn French's More Girls Who Do Comedy* was a spin-off series. Dawn French's *Boys Who Do Comedy* was the next series to air. Each program ended with a tribute to the late comic *Linda Smith.*

*Phyllis Diller, Catherine Tate, and Whoopi Goldberg* were just a few of the famous comics interviewed on *Dawn French's Boys Who Do Comedy.* Three programs included excerpts from French's interviews, while another six episodes had complete interviews. More Girls Who Do Comedy with Dawn French was a spinoff that was also broadcast on BBC Four. In 2007, Dawn French's Boys Who Do Comedy took over the comedy slot. Comedian Dawn French conducts in-depth interviews with the men she admires most in the comedy industry. In addition to her roles in *Agatha Christie's Marple* and *Lark Rise* to *Candleford,*

Dawn French also ventured into the world of comedy. She starred in a series consisting of three 30-minute episodes, where each episode focused on a different aspect of the characters' professional lives. The series offered a glimpse into the world of comedy, featuring footage of other renowned comedians from the past.

Furthermore, French hosted another show called *Dawn French's More Boys Who Do Comedy*. In this series, she engaged in conversations with well-known comedians such as *John Cleese, Graham Norton, Bill Bailey, Rob Brydon, Russell Brand, and Ken Dodd.* The show provided an opportunity for the French to delve deeper into the world of comedy by interviewing and discussing the craft with these talented individuals.

French, who replaced *Elizabeth Spriggs* as *The Fat Lady*, appeared in the film version of *Harry Potter* and the *Prisoner* of *Azkaban*. Though they didn't appear on screen together, *Lenny Henry*, who was then married to French, performed the voice of the Shrunken Head in the same picture.

French's career on the camera wasn't just centred on TV roles. *The Chronicles of Narnia, Love, and Other Disasters*, and others featured her in brief cameos. As *Miriam Forcible*, she provided her voice for the 2009 stop-motion dark fantasy film Coraline. Several other voice actors, including *Dakota Fanning* and *Jennifer*

*Saunders*, also participated. A little girl named *Coraline* (*Mandy Moore*) moves into a new house and soon finds a mysterious door leading to another world. The doppelgangers of her parents in this reality are all smiles and button eyes, but they hide a dark secret from her. Coraline must face this evil with the assistance of her pals and a stray black cat if she is to find and save her actual parents. With a global revenue of almost $324 million, the picture was a commercial and critical triumph. Its score and production values garnered several honors.

Towards the end of 2010, French landed a big part in the two-season NBC comedy *Roger & Val Have Just Got In*, costarring *Alfred Molina*. French and Alfred played the married couple *Roger and Val Stephenson* in the program created by French, which focused on the pair's mundane, daily problems. The hilarity follows them from the moment they enter through the door until thirty minutes later. Dawn French's performance as Val earned a nomination for a *BAFTA* for the program.

In the English version of the *German-British* environmental animated feature Animals United, the *Welsh* actress also provided her voice for the part of *Angie the Elephant.* The same year, French also made an appearance in the Christmastime short comedy film series *Little Crackers.*

She then became known for her role as *Midwife Joy Aston* in the nine-episode run of the psychological thriller series *Psychoville*. There are five main protagonists in the program, all of whom are English but have been blackmailed by the same individual. Each of them gets a letter that simply says, *I know what you did.* As the season goes on, the protagonists learn the shocking truth about a murder and their ties to a psychiatric institution. For marketing reasons, the program was dubbed *Psychoville* when it was marketed to Asian countries including Japan and Korea.

The British comedic talk program *The Paul O'Grady program* welcomed the French and Saunders actress as a guest in 2009. After that, in 2010, she was a guest on *Michael Bublé's Home For Christmas* as an honorary holiday spirit. In July 2012, she participated as a judge for *ITV*'s live Superstar competition. The goal of the UK talent competition was to identify the person who would play the title role in a stage adaptation of *Jesus Christ Superstar.* After a competitive process, *Ben Forster* was cast as *Jesus* for the UK arena tour, beating out *Rory Taylor.* The show's contestants were selected after auditioning in cities around the country and spending a week in intensive training on Superstar Island. *Andrew Lloyd Webber's* house in *Majorca* hosted the final rounds, while *Wembley,* England's Fountain Studios hosted the live concerts.

*Melanie C, Jason Donovan, Dawn French, and Andrew Lloyd Webber* were among the judges who deliberated before announcing a winner based on public voting.

In March 2013, it was revealed that French would be joining *Kyle Sandilands, Geri Halliwell* (who had previously replaced *Dannii Minogue*), and *Timomatic* as the judges on Australia's *Got Talent on the Nine Network.* French was replacing *Brian McFadden.* French left the program after just one season, and *Kelly Osbourne* took her place. Later, she played Frances for a few episodes in the British comedy show *Heading Out.* At the end of 2014, French toured the United Kingdom and Oceania with her autobiographical one-woman performance, *30 Million Minutes.* When the program was being made, she had already been alive for a certain number of minutes, and that number became the title.

From 2016 to 2019, French co-starred as the gifted cook Gina in the Sky 1 series *Delicious,* whose renowned chef ex-husband Leo (Iain Glen) has remarried and established a thriving hotel company with his new wife Sam (Emilia Fox) in Cornwall, and whom she is having an affair. In the pilot, Leo dies, yet he keeps popping up in people's thoughts and conversations. Leo, Gina, Leo's widow Sam, and their children all have difficult dynamics that are examined throughout the series. There will not be a Season 4 of the program, it was confirmed in June

2019. Some reviewers praised the show's plot and Dawn French's performances, while others panned it for having a cast that didn't mesh well together. Throughout 2016, it averaged 1.87 million viewers, making it Sky 1's most-viewed original drama.

She also appeared in 300 *Years of French and Saunders* and presented the British talent competition *Little Big Shots* in 2017.

In 2020, she co-starred with Mark Heap for six episodes of *The Trouble with Maggie Cole*. British comedy-drama series starring French as a local busybody and self-proclaimed historian Maggie Cole in the seaside town of Thurlbury. After spilling the beans on six residents of the village on the radio,

Maggie feels guilty and must deal with the repercussions. During the same period, she also contributed her voice to the TV documentary series *Cornwall Air 999* as its narrator. The television drama *Roald & Beatrix: The Tail of the Curious Mouse* featured her as the show's namesake character. Based on the real tale of Roald Dahl's encounter with Beatrix Potter when he was six years old, the film follows young Roald as he travels to England in search of the author who inspired him so much: Beatrix Potter. The film, directed by Dawn French and shot in Wales, was well-welcomed by critics and audiences alike. The title sequence was nominated for a BAFTA for its paper cutout animation style.

In 2021, French served as a celebrity guest judge on the second season of RuPaul's Drag Race UK, where she evaluated the comedic stand-up performances of the show's final five competitors: Lawrence Chaney, Bimini Bon-Boulash, Tayce, Ellie Diamond, and A'Whora.

On the musical game show *Walk The Line*, she was one of the judges. Barlow took over as the show's judge after Simon Cowell turned down the offer. However, in August of 2022, the show was terminated after just a single season. The final round of the competition included five musical artists fighting for a £500,000 grand prize. The winner of each show might either perform again the next night or cash in their winnings. The runner-up was allowed to continue in the game.

Still, in 2022, she played *Mrs. Bowers* in the film adaptation of *Agatha Christie's* 1937 mystery book *Death on the Nile*. *Hercule Poirot* is a detective in this film who solves a murder that happens on a wedding cruise down the Nile. The film opened to mixed reviews when it was released in many foreign regions in February 2022. Over its average expenditure of $95 million, it earned $137.3 million globally.

Her most recent projects include lending her voice to the character of *Mrs. Bowers* in *The Magician's Elephant*, an animated film.

She also has acting experience on the stage. Among the plays in which French has appeared are *My Brilliant Divorce, Smaller, and A Midsummer Night's Dream,* in which she portrayed *Hermia,* a schoolteacher who takes care of her crippled mother. In January of 2007, French appeared with *Natalie Dessay* and *Juan Diego Flórez* in *The Daughter of the Regiment (La fille du régiment) by Gaetano Donizetti* at London's Royal Opera House, Covent Garden. French played the role of the *Duchesse de Crackentorp.* The 2010 production of La Fille du règiment brought French back to Covent Garden and the play.

The London Palladium production of *Jack and the Beanstalk* starring French opened in December 2022.

That same year, she took her show *Dawn French is a Huge Twat* on the road in the United Kingdom. It was revealed in late 2022 that she will be touring the UK again in the autumn of 2023 with the same show, followed by performances in Australia in 2024.

## Other Career Engagements

In 1997, French was appointed as the spokesperson for Terry's Chocolate Orange, a role she held until August 2007. Despite the company's assertions that it was time to move on, some have speculated that her dismissal was motivated by their belief that she was an unattractive role model for America's growing obesity epidemic because of her size. It was the Welsh actress who remarked *It's not Terry's, it's mine* popular, and the company's thanks to her put an end to the rumors. They continued by saying that the campaign partnership had ended and that they were now engaged in separate endeavors.

French has been a brand spokesperson and wrote the best-selling epistolary autobiography, *Dear Fatty*. The book, published in 2008, is a compilation of letters to those who have had an impact on her life, such as her father and her long-time comedy partner Jennifer Saunders, whom she refers to as *Fatty*. From her childhood until her marriage to Lenny Henry and subsequent divorce in 2010, French's life is chronicled in this book via four photo parts and paragraphs.

The chapters are filled with heartfelt recollections of her childhood, her father's suicide when she was 20, her struggles to find her true calling, her beginnings as a comedian, her time with the comedy group The Comic Strip, her enormous success with French and Saunders, and her subsequent work on *The Vicar of Dibley*. Throughout the book, she describes her never-ending efforts to make contact with her musical heroes, such as The Monkees and Madonna.

It becomes clear that French's bold character and unyielding will have been crucial to her achievement of success as you read the book. She isn't afraid to roll up her sleeves and put in the effort necessary to succeed, but she also clearly knows how to have fun along the way.

Well-known for her part in *The Vicar of Dibley*, actress Dawn French has also been featured in commercials for Churchill Insurance. She collaborated with Bespoke Music to record her voice for multiple Greatest Hits Radio Station idents in 2019.

Marks & Spencer, a major British grocery store chain, cast French as their beautiful fairy lady in their 2021 Christmas food advertising. Tom Holland also voiced the business mascot, Percy Pig, who was brought back to life after being dormant for 29 years. French's fairy persona is seen in the primary advertisement, dropping her wand over a box with

Percy Pig packaging. Percy jumps out of the box as soon as the lid pops open. French then takes Percy on a tour of the store's festive food selections throughout the remainder of the commercial. In the 2022 M&S holiday commercial, Jennifer Saunders reprises her role as French's voice-over partner, *Duckie*. Together, they set out on a touching adventure to spread holiday happiness and promote M&S Food's 2022 Christmas offerings.

In 2017, Dawn French published her second nonfiction book, titled *Me. You.* It follows the popularity of her four books, *A Tiny Bit Marvellous* (2010), *Oh Dear Silvia* (2012), *According to Yes* (2015), and *Because of You* (2020). In fact, *Because of You* made the shortlist for the *Women's Prize in Fiction* in 2021.

To her daughter, stepdaughter, and mother, *Because of You* is a love letter, as Dawn French puts it. She says the book inspired her to create it because it forced her to. This fictional work follows two families, each with its own set of parents. In 2020, one couple celebrates the birth of a healthy daughter on New Year's Day, while another grieves the death of their unborn child. Hope, the mother who lost her daughter, is so distraught that she snatches the healthy baby from her sleeping husband and wife and calls her Minnie. Hope's husband, overcome with shame, abandons her to raise their daughter Minnie alone while he goes to live in the country of his origin in Africa.

In the meanwhile, *Anna and Julius*, the scheming politician, have their challenges as a pair. Anna's grief at her daughter's death is palpable, but Julius plans to use it for political gain. *Anna and Julius* separated some years later, and since then, Anna has avoided all touch with her ex-spouse. Minnie, who was brought up in a kind family but is now pregnant despite having heart difficulties, lives in an alternate universe. Doctors, whom Hope has avoided for a long time, begin to wonder about Minnie's lineage as a result of this. Hope's deepest, most kept secret will eventually be exposed.

The book is a remarkable piece of French writing, with a tale that is both moving and sophisticated while being considerably different from the author's earlier, lighter works. She freely stated that she knew nothing about the emotional struggles that accompany the miscarriage of a newborn. In October 2023, she will release The Twat Files, her third nonfiction book and a companion to her second stand-up special, *Dawn French is a Huge Twat*.

In 1986, the renowned British actress appeared in the music video Experiment IV for a song by Kate Bush, where she was joined by the equally impressive *Hugh Laurie, Richard Vernon, and Peter Vaughan. Alison Moyet's music videos for Love Letters (which also starred Saunders)* in 1987 and Whispering *Your Name* (also starring Saunders) in 1994 both included French.

French has donated her acting skills to not one, but two, shows for *Comic Relief*, in addition to showcasing them in music videos. With *Jennifer Saunders and Kathy Burke,* she formed the band Lananeeneenoonoo in 1989. A benefit single for *Comic Relief* was produced in collaboration with Bananarama. Released on the London Records label on 25 February 1989, the band's cover of *They Didn't Know* that Anastacia was eavesdropping on their talk from behind the stalls. Soon, French found herself wearing Anastacia's trademark cowgirl outfit and singing on Top of the Pops with the star. But she felt no happiness, only a crushing self-doubt. She had never felt so unattractive as she did at that moment. Meanwhile, on the UK Singles Chart, the song quickly rose to the top three positions. It spent an incredible nine weeks at the top spot. In 1997, French, Saunders, and Burke got back together for Comic Relief, this time performing as The Sugar Lumps. They sang a brilliant parody of The Spice Girls' Who Do You Think You Are with the great Llewella Gideon and Lulu.

## Cheers to the Wins

Both French and Saunders have been honored with several awards for their work. After being rated one of the 50 funniest performers in British comedy by

*The Observer* in 2003, French and her co-star received the prestigious *Golden Rose of Montreux* in 2002. In addition, a survey conducted in 2006 found that French was the celebrity in Britain's female population who was most adored. According to *BBC Radio 4's Woman's Hour*, French was included among the 100 most *powerful women* in the UK in 2013.

French and Saunders have garnered French several nominations for various honors throughout the years. As a result of her work *French and Saunders and The Vicar of Dibley*, she has been nominated for a *BAFTA TV Award*. Her roles in *The Vicar of Dibley, Ted and Alice, and Wild West* earned her nominations for *British Comedy Awards and National Television Awards*. She has also been honored with prizes including the *British Comedy Award and the Writers Guild of Great Britain Award* for TV-Light Entertainment for her work on *The Vicar of Dibley.*

Both French and Saunders turned down an OBE in 2001. The comic actresses felt they are being paid enough for their fun jobs and didn't want to share the spotlight with others who had devoted their lives to more deserving causes. In addition to French's 2009 *Annie Award* nomination for Voice Acting in a Feature Production for her role in *Coraline,* the team earned the *Rose d'Or Light Entertainment Festival Award* in 2002.

# Dawn's World

On the independent comic scene, French crossed paths with Lenny Henry. After seeing her act at a comedy club, Henry couldn't help but fall for her. Henry had been on a string of casual romances before he met French, but none of them had lasted. The majority of his past relationships had been driven by physical attraction, and he had a hard time maintaining interest in anybody for very long.

So, he was becoming more and more alone, yet he yearned for something more than loneliness. The situation changed drastically once he met French.

The best part of his talk with fellow comic Dawn French was that he didn't have to make her laugh at any point. Her ability to make him laugh was a welcome change, and he found it invigorating. That's when he knew he was more than just friends with Dawn. Henry's political convictions, as well as countless other things, were clarified via their in-depth discussions and mutual interests. Their sense of humour helped them through difficult times and brought them closer together. Finally, he realized that he was getting emotionally attached to her.

They tied the knot on October 20, 1984, in *London's Covent Garden*. In his autobiography, Henry writes that he and his wife always planned to have a big, fancy wedding to prove to their friends and family that they were for real. He insisted that they not get married until it was a big, fancy ceremony with all the trimmings. *Billie*, their daughter, was adopted by the couple. French claims that Billie has always been aware that she was adopted, but that she filed for an injunction to prevent the name of Billie's original mother from being revealed. When asked how she and Henry would feel if Billie expressed interest in locating her biological mother, French said they would be totally on board with the idea. She is concerned, though, that someone else may choose Billie.

Henry is a well-known British comedian, actor, and writer, lauded for his extensive repertoire of personas. As his career progressed, he took on more serious parts. In addition, Henry was instrumental in creating and presenting the British version of Comic Relief.

When Henry was 16 he made it big on the TV talent show *New Faces* after years of honing his humorous skills in local nightclubs as a teenager. *The Fosters* (1976–1977), the first British situation comedy with an all-black ensemble, gave him his first taste of mainstream success. Henry then had several cameo appearances on other television programs after this success, including traditional children's shows like

Tiswas and more experimental shows like The Young Ones.

Henry was given his program by the BBC in 1984, which he appropriately titled *The Lenny Henry Show*. The presentation included both stand-up and skits, with Henry playing a wide variety of offbeat characters with catchy one-liners. His impersonations, although generally well-received, were criticized for allegedly promoting racist stereotypes. Henry reflected on this and admitted that some of his positions were damaging to him. The program was a hit, although it was canceled and revived many times, including being recast as a fake comedy for a year from 1987 to 1988.

Henry founded *Crucial Films*, his production firm, in 1991. In the same year, he made his Hollywood debut as the lead in the critically and commercially unsuccessful picture *True Identity*.

Henry returned to the spotlight in the cult classic situation *comedy Chef!*, which aired on the BBC in 1993 and ran for three years. In 1993, due to his exceptional work, he was named BBC Personality of the Year by the Radio and Television Industry Club. Henry wanted to broaden his acting experience, so he accepted a serious role in a BBC series called *Hope and Glory* (1999–2000), which led to supporting roles in films like *Harry Potter and the Prisoner of Azkaban* (2004) *and MirrorMask* (2005).

Henry's performance as a greengrocer and possible suspect in *Broadchurch's* last season (2017) demonstrated his acting range. Three years later, in the first episodes of Doctor Who's twelfth season, he wowed viewers once again. Henry has hosted the annual Comic Relief telethon since its inception in 1988. Just like its American equivalent, comedians performed at this telethon to raise money for a good cause. Soon after the organization's annual fund-raising event, Red Nose Day, became widely publicized, Henry became one of the most known faces connected with it.

Henry had his theatrical debut in the main role of Othello by *William Shakespeare* in 2009 at the *West Yorkshire Playhouse* in Leeds, and he did an outstanding job. The plaudits for his performance were so good that the show was moved to London's prestigious West End. Henry also won praise for his performance as *Troy Maxson* in a 2013 staging of *August Wilson's Fences*. Henry's efforts in the creative sector have not been ignored. It was in 1999 when he achieved the esteemed rank of Commander of the British Empire (CBE). He later earned the title of a Knight bachelor.

Dawn French was widely reported to be a *Labour Party voter* during the 2010 election campaign. Her political beliefs were reinforced by her support for Keir Starmer in the 2020 Labour leadership race.

French and her ex-husband Lenny Henry formally announced their divorce on April 6, 2010, after a 25-year marriage. Their divorce was reportedly cordial even though they were previously married. They decided to split up back in October of the year before, but they didn't make it public because they were still haggling over the divorce details. Later that year, they formalized their divorce. French and Henry have, remarkably, remained amicable throughout their breakup.

Lenny and Dawn seldom talk about why they decided to divorce, however, Lenny did say that one spouse generally wanted to leave the marriage more than the other. They eventually realized that being together was impossible and broke up. Lenny denounced the infidelity claims strongly when they were circulating. It was pointed out, however, that they had been diverging long before they broke up.

In 2011, Dawn French, who had previously been divorced, started dating Mark Bignell, an executive at a charitable organization. Their romance flourished, and they were married on April 22, 2013. Therapist *Mark Bignell and Dawn's* late mother co-founded the nonprofit *Hamoaze House.* Rehabilitating alcoholics and drug addicts back into mainstream society is the main goal of this group. The organization also opened a shop in Plymouth's West Hoe neighborhood in 2018. Mark Bignell has two children from his previous marriages, a daughter and a son.

Dawn and Mark first connected through Roma French, Dawn's late mother, who created the organization where Mark currently serves as CEO. Mark had to ask who she was when they first met. Dawn wasn't in the market for romance at the moment. At first, she prepared herself for a life of solitude and even welcomed it. She wasn't in the market for a new love interest or a confidante. The couple settled in a mansion in Fowey, Cornwall, with views of Readymoney Cove.

This 19th-century structure, designated as Grade II, has stood the test of time. French sold her Fowey home in May 2021 and relocated to a Calstock mansion built in the Gothic revival style in 1868. Three times what she paid for it in 2006, she sold her cherished Fowey property in 2021 for £6.6 million. French was appointed as Falmouth University's new chancellor in September 2014. French is an avid Plymouth Argyle fan.

## Teenage Dawn French

At the age of 16, Dawn had never been sexually active. For her, this was hardly a child's play. Her mind was always awash in sexy fantasies. There was a good chance that she was fantasizing about, hoping for, dreading, or desiring it. She fell in love with each of her brother's buddies individually since she was at a girls' school while he was at a boys' school. Most of the time, these feelings were directed at the wrong persons. She wondered daily when that last day would arrive. She would perfect her pucker by kissing plums, other girls, and cushions. The optimistic spirit of the younger French was present in every situation. Surprisingly, she hasn't changed at all in height.

There was a time when French teenagers lacked self-assurance. She had many ups and downs, but her father was always there to steady him. One night she went out in her purple suede hot pants and had an experience she will never forget. He made an effort to tell her how much he appreciated her beauty and worth. He said he'd be completely crushed if anything bad happened to her. He reassured her that anybody she chose to date would be very fortunate. Her dad knew she was feeling insecure as she headed out the door to their celebration. To her credit, she did trust him, and she carried with her the enduring effects of her father's vote of confidence. She considers herself lucky to have had a father who always believed in her and whose words she continues to believe to be true.

Dawn's father committed suicide when she was 18 years old. It was unclear to her at the time how she had come to experience such profound trauma. She battled feelings of rage, bewilderment, and despair, often projecting the blame for her emotional distress onto others. But as time went on, she learned more about mental health and understood that things may have been different if her father hadn't been embarrassed by his sadness. Having matured, she now knows that it is possible to forgive and have compassion for one's father since she understands that he was seeking his way out at the time.

She now understands that period of his life was a living horror for him. Her father seemed quite different to her now, and she noticed it. Age brought the realization that she, too, was heading on that path. She worried and felt overwhelmed when she took on new obligations, such as raising children and paying debts. Though she was overjoyed to become a mother, she soon realized that the burden of duty was too much. Since then, she has chosen to alter her lifestyle and adopt a more optimistic point of view.

Dawn thinks her younger self would be quite proud of the comedic career she has built for herself.

She would choose to have that last discussion with her father if she could. She feels like she has him in her back pocket at all times, so she is surprised that she would want to speak to him about his mental health problems. Though others did, and it was considered rude to discuss them, she knew nothing about them. Generally speaking, he was a fun-loving, humorous, adventurous, and upbeat father. Sometimes he would retreat to a dark room, but she would always chalk it up to a migraine. She'd want to have a conversation with him now that she has a better grasp of the situation.

Dawn would most want to revisit the time when she was 18 years old. At the time, she was camping in a tent on the dunes above Gwithian Sands, a beach in

Cornwall. Everything she had worried about for years came true in that private time in the tent with the charming guy she had just met. It was all cozy. In the end, they created a happy memory as they spent time together, kissed, swam, and shared a Fab ice lolly by the ocean.

# The Health Threat

The star's health and weight became the subject of speculation when she shed an astounding seven and a half stones. In 2011, she received the news that she had uterine cancer. Dawn's weight loss before her hysterectomy allowed her surgeons to do keyhole surgery and shorten her recuperation time, leading some to speculate that she had a gastric band installed. It was a bold move on the part of a celebrity to get the operation, considering thereafter ladies are unable to become pregnant. But at 64 years old and after a lifetime of uterine problems, Dawn felt ready to go through with the procedure.

The cancer fear that led physicians to suspect that Dawn had uterine cancer was a major factor in their decision to do the procedure. She checked herself into the hospital, where her doctor promptly ordered a second biopsy to double-check the results of the first. She had already made up her mind to end her pregnancy before learning the outcome of the second.

A hysterectomy is defined as a treatment in which the uterus is surgically removed to alleviate symptoms of disease or dysfunction affecting the female reproductive system. She needed to lose weight so that her recuperation period after surgery would be less than a couple of months.

In 2022, she discussed a terrible health crisis during which she was unable to stand properly and felt as if her skull was caving inwards.

She endured terrible vertigo on her previous tour, leading doctors to fear a brain tumor. She felt like she was on a boat and couldn't tell which way was up, so she brought a walking stick on the stage with her. Investigations revealed that the intense spotlights on the stage were the cause of her symptoms. Her mind had a hard time adjusting to the opposites of light and dark. Her condition was exacerbated by the slanted stage. At the moment, Dawn is in finer shape than normal.

Osteoarthritis is a painful ailment that affects the joints and may cause stiffness; in August 2023, Dawn French provided an insight into what it's like to experience osteoarthritis. The famous actress has spoken openly about her *crumbly knee* and shared photos of the workouts she was doing to treat it. French also discussed her RA in a December 2020 interview. Rheumatoid arthritis is an inflammatory illness that affects the immune system and several joints, while osteoarthritis often starts in a single joint and tears away the smooth cartilage there. Although it is not known for sure, French may suffer from both rheumatoid arthritis and osteoarthritis.

Whatever the issue may be, French have consistently shown to be strong and courageous in the face of any health crises.

# Facts

- Her strong passion is to help curvy women dress stylishly, and she has achieved this by collaborating on knitting books and opening a boutique with affordable and fashionable items. Initially, she aimed to pursue a career in theatre education and become a drama teacher.

- In the revived series of *Doctor Who* in 2017, *Tom Baker*, a renowned character from the original show, proposed French for the role of the *Doctor*. He found her intriguing and appreciated her sharp sense of humor.

- During a romantic gondola ride in Venice, her current husband, Mark Bignell, proposed to her.

- In 1961, *Queen Elizabeth The Queen Mother* visited Sgt. Denys French and his family at *RAF Leconfield* where she met Dawn, Sgt. French's daughter who was three years and nine months old at the time. This encounter was later included in Dawn's video/comedy tour called *Thirty Million Minutes.*

- Both Dawn and her adopted daughter Billie share the middle name Roma as a tribute to Dawn's mother, Felicity Roma.

- She, along with Imelda Staunton and Billy Connolly, declined roles in a 1998 Peter Greenaway film because it required full nudity on screen.

# Summary

Dawn French, a Welsh actress and author, was born on October 11, 1957, in Holyhead. She is known for her work in television comedy series, particularly her partnership with *Jennifer Saunders* on the groundbreaking show *French and Saunders*. French and Saunders first met in the late 1970s at *London's Central School of Speech and Drama*. Their strong connection was evident in the skits they created together, fueled by their shared passion for performance. They reunited in 1980 as cast members of the Comic Strip, a renowned comedy club in London, marking the beginning of a highly productive collaboration. Their talent and charm quickly caught the attention of television producers, leading to roles in various Comic Strip projects and French's successful series, Girls on Top. However, in 1987, French and Saunders embarked on their adventure as the writers and stars of their sketch comedy show, also titled *French and Saunders.*

Dawn French's solo career took off with the comedy-drama series *Murder Most Horrid*, in which she starred from 1991 to 1999. During this time, she showcased her acting skills and gained recognition. In 1993, French made a memorable impression with her exceptional performance in the BBC drama *Tender Loving Care.* However, it was her portrayal of the title character in the TV series *The Vicar of Dibley* in 1994 that catapulted her to stardom. The show became a huge success and continued running until 2007, solidifying French's place as a beloved and talented actress.

Between 1995 and 2003, French was not only a writer for Saunders' acclaimed series *Fabulous* but also made guest appearances. She subsequently starred in many additional high-profile TV shows as a starring character. The BBC's Ted and Alice (2002), a romantic comedy, was one of them. In 2006, French and Saunders teamed up again for the wonderful comedy Jam & Jerusalem (released in the US under the title Clatterford). The next year, in A Bucket o'

French and Saunders, the hilarious duo returned to the big screen.

*The Wrong Mans* (2013–14), a highly respected comedy co-created by James Corden, joins the critically acclaimed costume drama Lark Rise to Candleford (2008–2011) as part of French's outstanding television repertory. Her 2016 project, Delicious, had her playing an ex-wife having an affair with her new husband. In 2017, the program 300 Years of French and Saunders was shown on television. In 2020, French had the main part in The Trouble with Maggie Cole, a show about a lady who is always spreading rumors.

Dawn French also had a career on Broadway. As Bottom in 2001's *A Midsummer Night's Dream*, she demonstrated her acting chops. Two years later, she wowed the crowds with the one-woman show *My Brilliant Divorce*. In 2014, French pushed her talents to the next level with the premiere of her solo stand-up show, *30 Million Minutes*, which toured Great Britain and Australia to widespread critical acclaim. Most notably, she played the Wicked Queen in *Snow White* at London's renowned Palladium from 2018 to 2019.

French's acting prowess was not limited to the theater; she also took on film roles. Books like *Harry Potter and the Prisoner of Azkaban* (2004) and *Love and Other Disasters* (2006) stand out. She also provided her voice for characters in *Coraline* (2009) and *The Chronicles of Narnia: The Lion, the Witch, and the Wardrobe* (2005). French's film career has featured a few modest roles and an executive producer credit for 2016's *Absolutely Fabulous: The Movie*. She also landed a part in the planned 2022 film version of Agatha Christie's Death on the Nile, directed by Kenneth Branagh.

French is well-known not just for her acting roles, but also as the co-founder (together with Helen Teague) of Sixteen 47, a company that sells fashionable apparel for women of larger sizes. She married Comic Relief co-founder and performer Lenny Henry in 1984. French's love for the arts prompted her to become chancellor at Cornwall's Falmouth University the same year (2015). She published many publications that displayed her writing abilities, including the biography Dear Fatty (2008). French has written a total of six novels, the most recent of which came out in October under the title The Twat Files.

With her new stand-up performance, Dawn French is a Huge Twat, Dawn will be coming to New Zealand in May. As part of her travels, she will stop in Auckland, Wellington, and Christchurch.

Printed in Great Britain
by Amazon

35125276R00057